A Rise to Clarity

Quitting Marijuana and learning to live a happy life without it

By Jason Jackson

A RISE TO CLARITY - A GUIDE TO QUITTING MARIJUANA AND LEARNING TO LIVE A HAPPY LIFE WITHOUT IT

First edition. March 28, 2024.

ISBN: 979-8224861699

Written by Jason Jackson.

A Rise to Clarity

Quitting marijuana and learning to live a happy life without it.

By Jason Jackson

Chapter Index

Introduction

Quitting marijuana usage can be a daunting task, but the benefits to your physical and mental health, as well as your bank account, are *immense*. This book is designed to help you quit *immediately* and experience the many advantages of a THC-free lifestyle. From improved cognitive function to increased productivity, the rewards of quitting marijuana are numerous and life-changing.

One of the most significant benefits of quitting marijuana is the mental *clarity* it brings. I dub this the "***Rise to Clarity***" - this phenomenon occurs when the body is finally free from the effects of the drug, allowing for sharper focus, quicker reactions, and improved decision-making skills. No longer will you be weighed down by the foggy haze with slow reaction times, you'll experience this *Rise to Clarity* that will enable you to tackle tasks and personal relationships in ways you never thought you could. You might be such a long-time user that you don't even remember what it is like to be sober. Some describe the experience after quitting as "Feeling Superhuman". Are you ready for a sharp body and mind again?

This book is divided into ten chapters, each one tackling a different aspect of marijuana habit breaking. From withdrawal symptoms and managing cravings to dealing with social pressures and solving boredom, this book covers all the critical components of quitting marijuana for good.

Prepare for your **RISE TO CLARITY**.

Chapter 1: Why Quit?

Reason #1 to Quit - Your body will appreciate it.

Smoking, vaping, and even edibles are all associated with dozens of negative physical effects. Trouble with your lungs, heart, immune system, sleep, as well as increased chance of cancers and diabetes are all linked to long-term use. Every aspect of your body from your head to your feet will be improved by quitting marijuana/THC usage. Yes, that's right! Your brain function will be sharper, your skin will become more clear, and your energy levels will soar. Plus, you'll be reducing the risk of all those nasty illnesses mentioned earlier and dozens more.

Do you regularly cough or have a persistent cough?

The first reason to quit marijuana is the effect it has on your lungs. Inhaling any substance is harmful, but when you smoke or vape weed, you're inhaling tar and other carcinogens that can lead to lung cancer. Yes, even when vaping. Smoking marijuana irritates airways and causes chronic bronchitis. Most marijuana smokers and vapers develop a persistent cough. It could be such a common occurrence to you that you don't even realize you do it all day anymore. This will disappear. Not only will your lungs and throat appreciate not coughing, but so will your muscles, and all of the people around you. When you quit you will have less phlegm production, and the improvement in lung function will give you greater stamina throughout the day (and night!).

Does your sleep suffer?

It is common knowledge that getting a good night's sleep is important. Poor sleep is known to cause depression and eating disorders. Marijuana use has been shown to disrupt sleep patterns, leading to difficulty falling asleep, staying asleep, and experiencing restful REM sleep. By quitting marijuana you will experience improved sleep quality and increased energy levels during the day, as adequate sleep is essential for maintaining good physical and mental health.

Better Digestive Health

Long-term THC consumption is associated with gastrointestinal issues such as chronic abdominal pain, nausea, and diarrhea. By limiting the harmful effects of smoke on the respiratory system, when you quit you will experience an improvement in all digestive functions such as appetite and metabolism. This can lead to a healthier weight and improved nutrient absorption, further contributing to better overall health. Not to mention that edibles often contain diabetes-causing amounts of sugar.

A Better Memory / Sharper Mind

Studies have shown that individuals who quit smoking cannabis experienced an improvement in their memory and cognitive abilities within just one week - and the improvements in memory and cognitive abilities continue to progress in the weeks following. Another study found that individuals who abstained from cannabis use for one month showed significant improvement in their verbal memory and working memory compared to those who continued using it.

Reason #2 to Quit - Your budget will appreciate it.

You or someone you know is not only buying marijuana, but also the shipping or travel costs go go get it. This can add up over time to tremendous amounts. By quitting you will significantly reduce your financial strain, freeing up a substantial amount of money that would have otherwise been spent on THC products. This extra cash can then be used to build a large investment account, pay off debts, or purchase new items that you've been wanting or putting off.

For example, you could use the money saved from not buying marijuana to save for an emergency fund, which can provide financial security and peace of mind in case of unexpected events such as job loss or medical emergencies. You could also use this money to make a down payment on or outright purchase a car, house, or even start a business- helping you achieve greater long-term financial goals. You could use the money to plan a trip to another state or country, attend concerts, cruises, or vacations, or buy life-changing gifts for parents and loved ones.

Quitting marijuana allows you to prioritize your spending and allocate your funds towards more meaningful and fulfilling activities. Instead of spending your money on THC products, you can invest in hobbies, take classes, or enrich your life and the lives of those around you. The possibilities are endless when you choose to quit marijuana and redirect your resources towards more important things.

Realistically, by spending money on marijuana, you are robbing yourself of tips, vacations, and life-changing 'upgrades' like cars and improved housing, and more...

Reason #3 to Quit - Your relationships will grow.

Quitting marijuana will lead to significant improvements in your relationships with family, friends, and coworkers. It impairs communication, motivation, emotional stability, and memory. As the THC leaves your system, you will be able to start to remember people's names, dates, places, numbers, all things that would normally disappear out of a marijuana user's mind. Your communication skills will increase, and your relationships will improve as a result.

It is well documented that marijuana use leads to misunderstandings and miscommunications with loved ones. By quitting marijuana, individuals can improve their verbal and non-verbal communication skills, fostering better understanding and connection with others. Clearer communication can also help resolve conflicts more easily and promote healthier relationships.

Improved Emotional Stability: Chronic marijuana use has been linked to mood disorders and difficulties regulating emotions. By quitting marijuana, you will experience greater emotional stability, leading to more stable and consistent interactions with others. This improved emotional regulation will result in fewer arguments, less volatility, and increased trust within relationships.

Greater Motivation and Engagement: Marijuana leads to decreased motivation and engagement in activities, hobbies, and social events. Quitting marijuana will reignite your passion for life, allowing you to participate more fully in the lives of those around you. Increased involvement in shared activities will strengthen relationships and create new memories, further enriching connections with friends and loved ones. This is an important part of living your life to the fullest!

As you rediscover your passions and values, you will find your relationships to be more authentic, supportive, and nurturing. This newfound *clarity* will lead to healthier relationships, increased self-awareness, and a greater appreciation for the people who matter most in your life.

Reason #4 to Quit - You will grow

By eliminating the negative effects of marijuana use on your brain, emotions, and overall well-being, you will find that you will develop a stronger sense of identity and purpose, leading to a more fulfilling and meaningful life.

Quitting marijuana enhances self-awareness, which is a crucial aspect of personal growth. Marijuana use clouds judgment and impairs decision-making skills, making it difficult for individuals to recognize and understand their thoughts, emotions, and behaviors. In contrast, sobriety allows for greater *clarity* and insight into one's inner world, enabling you to to identify patterns, triggers, and areas for improvement in their lives. This heightened awareness will lead to better self-reflection, introspection, and personal development, as you become more attuned to their needs, desires, and values, and personal identity.

Quitting marijuana will increase your resilience, which is essential for navigating life's challenges and setbacks. Marijuana use leads to dependency, apathy, and avoidance, hindering an your ability to cope with stress and adversity. Abstaining from marijuana will allow you to build mental fortitude and stamina, enabling you to confront difficulties head-on, learn from mistakes, and bounce back from failures. As a result, you will be more adaptable, flexible, and capable of handling life's obstacles, ultimately becoming more resilient and empowered.

Quitting marijuana frees up mental and physical energy for more productive pursuits. Marijuana use can siphon off valuable resources, leaving you feeling lethargic, uninspired, and disconnected from your goals. In contrast, sobriety enables you to harness your potential, tap into your creativity, and engage in activities that promote personal growth. With renewed vigor and focus, you can explore new interests, acquire new skills, and pursue passions that enrich your life and foster self-improvement.

There's no doubt you will be more sharp in your mind. This enhanced emotional intelligence will lead to better relationships, increased self-esteem, and greater overall happiness.

"You are stronger than you think."

Chapter 2: What Clarity feels like

When an you stop smoking marijuana and ingesting THC, a series of transformative changes begin to take place within your mind and body. There will come a time when *'moments of clarity'* begin to emerge. These instances of mental acuity will leave you in awe - you'll find yourself recalling information with ease or reacting more quickly than before - improving both mentall and physical dexterity. It will feel as if the gears in your brain have been oiled and are now operating at lightning speed compared to their previous state during your THC haze. The improvement in cognitive function will be both noticeable and refreshing. You may feel superhuman! Day by day, as the effects of THC wear off, your brain's gears will start to turn more efficiently, enabling you to process information more quickly and accurately than before. Your mind will return to being a well-oiled machine operating at peak performance!

The moments of clarity that you experience during your THC abstinence will not only improve your cognitive function but also have a profound impact on other aspects of your life. You'll find yourself more focused and attentive in your daily tasks, making better decisions with greater efficiency. The enhanced mental state will allow you to tap into your creativity in ways never before possible while under the influence of THC. Your relationships will strengthen as communication becomes clearer and emotions are more easily expressed without clouding judgment.

"You have the strength to change your life."

Chapter 3: Preparing to quit

One critical aspect of preparing to quit is setting a firm date to stop using marijuana entirely. "Quit today" should become your mantra, as delaying the process can lead to procrastination, excuses, and ultimately failure. By choosing a specific day to begin your journey towards *clarity*, you demonstrate commitment, resolve, and determination to break free from the grip of THC.

Another essential consideration when preparing to quit is discretion. Deciding not to tell anyone about your decision can help you maintain focus and avoid unnecessary distractions or pressures. While sharing your intentions with trusted friends or family members can provide support and encouragement, discussing your plan with casual acquaintances or coworkers may lead to unwanted attention, skepticism, or even ridicule. By keeping your decision to quit private, you can create a protective bubble around your Rise to Clarity and guarantee success. Ultimately, this is *your* journey, not theirs.

It's important to identify and remove triggers from your routine that you would find too tempting to resist. If you often go to a particular place where marijuana is sold or used, you should try to change your routine to avoid being near it. Cravings are a normal part of the quitting process, and they can be particularly intense during the first few weeks after stopping use. It's essential to have strategies in place to manage these cravings when they arise.

An effective way to handle cravings is to engage in a distracting activity. This could be anything from going for a walk, calling a friend, or engaging in a hobby. By keeping your mind occupied, you can reduce the intensity of the craving and prevent yourself from giving in to the temptation to use.

One of the most significant challenges faced by individuals attempting to quit marijuana is navigating social situations where THC may be present or offered. Peer pressure and the fear of being judged or laughed at can make it difficult to resist using it, even after making a firm decision to quit. However, with assertiveness, preparation, and practice, it's possible to effectively respond to social pressure without drawing attention, and maintain your commitment to *clarity*.

When you find yourself in a situation where someone offers you marijuana, it's essential to have some useful phrases at the ready that will help you decline the offer without causing any unwanted attention or trouble. Here are some different ways to say "no" to marijuana, each one meant to be polite, respectful, and clear in its message:

"No thanks"

"Im good, just not today"

"I don't feel like it now, thanks"

"Another time"

"Ive got stuff to do I want a clear mind for"

"Ive had enough for today, thanks"

"Ive got an early start tomorrow, no thank you"

"I've got other plans I need to be sober for, thanks"

"The medicine I'm on doesn't go well with weed"

"Ive got a headache, I'm good"

"Another time, just not now"

"Ive got things to do"

"Ive gotta work"

"Doesn't work good on my meds"

"Im on a tolerance break"

"I gotta get up early tomorrow"

"Maybe later"

"Im not in the mood to smoke now, thanks"

"Pass, thanks"

They don't need to know the details of if you've quit it or how long you've quit it, you can just deny the marijuana and move on. It's important to remember that you don't owe anyone an explanation or detailed reasoning of your decision. Simply denying the use of marijuana and moving on from the conversation is a valid option.

"Your past does not define your
future - every moment is a chance for
a new beginning."

Chapter 4: Quitting for good

If there is one chapter you should read, this is it. This is your guide to quitting. Marijuana / THC dependence is simply an addiction of *habit*. Once you break the *habit* your mind will soon stop thinking about it and wanting it. Once you get past the initial hurdles, you will notice improvements in your enhanced memory and focus. You will also find yourself more motivated and productive, and your overall health will improve as you reduce your intake and increase your physical activity levels. It's generally two weeks of withdrawal symptoms, and then smooth sailing from there.

Method #1 - The Travel Distraction

The #1 proven most successful way to do this is to go on a trip out of town, where you wont and can't have access to marijuana products - for two *weeks*. This is a proven method because in addition to not having any marijuana, you will be distracted while visiting the out of town places. The primary vector of addiction in marijuana is simply one of *routine and environment.* That's where *The Roadtrip* comes in. By taking a trip out of town for at least two weeks, you're removing yourself from the people, places, and things that have been associated with your marijuana use. This distance allows you to create a physical and mental separation from the habit, making it easier to break.

Additionally, traveling provides a great opportunity to distract yourself with new experiences and adventures. Visiting new places, meeting new people, and trying new activities can all help take your mind off of marijuana and onto more positive and fulfilling pursuits. Simply because you won't have access to it while you're away, you'll be able to give your body and mind a much-needed reset and cleansing from THC.

Ideally pick a destination is marijuana-free. Once you have chosen a marijuana-free destination, plan ahead for activities that will keep you engaged and entertained throughout your visit. Plan somewhere you can stay and visit museums, sporting events, a concert out of town, local parks and new businesses to distract yourself for two weeks. Trying new activities is also a crucial part of the travel experience that can help take your mind off of marijuana and onto more positive and constructive pursuits. Engaging in physical activities such as hiking, swimming, or biking can improve your health, and help clear out your lungs of all the stuff you have been inhaling, while providing a natural high that is far more satisfying than any substance. Learning new skills, such as cooking, painting, or dancing, can boost your confidence and creativity, giving you a sense of accomplishment and pride.

Method #2 - Tapering off / The Slow Quit

This method is wonderful because it helps your body to re-adapt slowly and your withdrawal symptoms will be minimal. You should notice a far less impact on your sleep and appetite if you do it this way.

This more gradual approach to quitting marijuana is especially helpful if you have been using THC for an extended period or at high doses. The idea behind this method is to slowly reduce your intake over time, giving your body and mind the chance to adjust to the decreasing levels of THC in your system.

To begin, you would start by consuming your usual amount of marijuana on the first day. It's essential to keep track of how much you are ingesting so that you can gradually decrease the dose each day. On the second day, you would commit to using slightly less than you did on the first day, and continue this pattern until you reach zero marijuana intake. When you run out, you don't buy more marijuana, and you will soon reach *clarity*.

Here are some examples journal entries you could use:

Day 1 - Smoked 5 joints

Day 2 - Smoked 4 joints

Day 3 - Smoked 3 and 1/2 of a joint

Day 4 - Rest day, didn't smoke

Day 5 - 2 joints

Day 6 - Ran out, Done.

Or for edibles:

Day 1: Ate 3 gummies Day 6: 0.75 gummies

Day 2: 2.5 gummies Day 7: Rest day (no THC)

Day 3: 2 gummies Day 8: 0.5 gummies

Day 4: 1.5 gummies Day 9: 0.25 gummies

Day 5: 1 gummies Day 10: 0 gummies (out)

Similarly for vape pens, you can count how many *puffs* you inhale. Go through your normal day, count the puffs, then do less the next day.

<u>The most important next step</u>: When you are *out*, you do not buy any more! No resupplies. *Clarity is within reach!*

<u>Method #3 - Cold Turkey / Immediate</u>

This is the hardest way to do it, but for the determined, you will have great success. You simply need to break the habit of smoking or ingesting THC for *two weeks*, and then never resupply yourself. The only reason this is the most difficult way to quit is because the withdrawal symptoms will hit you the hardest. Your sleep and appetite will be greatly impacted. You may even feel sick or like you have a cold or flu, this is a common side effect. Power through it.

Here is a timeline of symptoms most will experience during your first two weeks of stopping marijuana usage. If you make it to the 14 day mark, you will be all clear.

<u>Day 1-7:</u>

• Sleep changes: It is common to experience difficulty sleeping during the first few days after quitting marijuana. This may include trouble falling asleep or staying asleep. Vivid dreams and nightmares are also common during this time.

• Physical symptoms: Withdrawal symptoms such as headaches, sweating, shakiness, and nausea may occur during the first few days.

• Mood changes: You may experience mood swings, irritability, anxiety, and depression during the early stages of withdrawal.

• Cravings: As the body adjusts to being without marijuana, intense cravings for the drug may arise. These cravings can be triggered by various stimuli and can be challenging to overcome.

• Focus and concentration difficulties: During this time, cognitive function may still be affected, making it difficult to focus, concentrate, and remember things.

To help cope during this time: Increase your exercise. If you go to bed exhausted physically, you are more likely to sleep well. Many people drink various teas to help them relax as well. Try some tea an hour before bedtime.

Day 8-10:

•Appetite changes: By this point, most people will have experienced some level of appetite change. Some may notice that their appetite has decreased, while others may find themselves craving certain foods more than usual.

• Social withdrawal: It is common to feel uncomfortable around others during this time, and engaging in activities that were once enjoyable may seem daunting. This will go away as your body returns to normal.

Day 11-21:

• Anxiety and paranoia: Withdrawal from marijuana can lead to heightened feelings of anxiety and paranoia, which may peak around day 11 or 12 and subside by day 21.

• Emotional instability: The emotional rollercoaster that comes with quitting marijuana may continue to be present during this period, including rapid mood swings and overly emotional responses to situations.

After 21 Days:

• Most physical symptoms should have dissipated by this point, and any lingering discomfort should be manageable.

- Cravings may still arise, but they should be less intense than during the initial stages of withdrawal.

- Cognitive function should return to normal, and focus, concentration, and memory should improve.

- Mood stabilization: Emotions should become stable, and you should start 'feeling more like yourself' again.

"Addiction is a prison,
recovery is the key to freedom."

Chapter 5: Managing withdrawal

To cope with withdrawal, it is essential to have a variety of strategies in place. Here are some suggestions:

Healthy Snacks - You will be having appetite changes and cravings. Resupplying yourself with a stock of healthy snacks - opting for fruits, vegetables, and nuts can stabilize your blood sugar and reduce cravings.

Stay Hydrated - You're supposed to drink approximately 1 gallon / 128oz of water a day. Keeping hydrated helps alleviate many withdrawal symptoms and helps your body flush out the toxins in your body as you *rise to clarity*.

Drink Herbal Tea - Tea can you fall asleep or relax during times of stress. Other herbal teas, such as ginger or peppermint, can be beneficial. Additionally, they contain things like magnesium or vitamin B complex which aid in reducing anxiety and improving energy levels.

Omega-3 - These healthy fats are found in fish oil and play a crucial role in brain function and mood regulation. It is known to reduce symptoms of anxiety and depression.

Smaller more frequent meals - This can help with regulating your hunger as your digestive system begins to re-balance itself without THC. One of the most common symptoms is a fluctuation in appetite and hunger levels, which can be managed by consuming smaller and more frequent meals throughout the day. Consuming smaller and more frequent meals can help regulate your hunger as your digestive system begins to re-balance itself without THC. This approach provides a consistent supply of energy and nutrients to your body, preventing the sudden spikes and crashes that can occur when eating larger, less frequent meals. This strategy also helps reduce nausea and vomiting, two common symptoms associated with THC withdrawal.

Exercise & Exhaustion - It cannot be stressed enough.... If you are exercising and keeping your activity up, this will help overcome sleep and diet withdrawal symptoms.

Sleep Schedule and Routine - Having specific times that you go to bed and wake up will help you to fall asleep and wake up rested. This is a good time to condition your body to a set sleep schedule. In addition, having a routine, such as taking a bubble bath or shower before bed, meditating, or reading a book will calm you and build the foundation for regular sleep, and positive dreams.

Flu-like symptoms, such as headache, nausea, chills, and muscle pains are a common withdrawal symptoms of quitting THC. Over the counter pain relievers such as Tylenol / Ibuprofen / Paracetamol can all be used to help alleviate the symptoms, with a recommended dose being 1/2 what the bottle recommends. These medications can help to reduce fever and ease pain, making it easier for you to manage their symptoms and continue with the detox process. Have a good blanket with you in case you get the chills, and be ready to stop down when you get the sweats.

"Your dreams are valid - pursue them
with unwavering determination."

Chapter 6: You will dream again

One of the most curious aspects of daily marijuana usage people report is that they don't dream anymore. You probably can't remember when you last dreamed, or you've forgotten that nightly dreaming is *normal*. When you quit putting THC in your body, your first few dreams are usually very vivid and very realistic. Eventually your dreams will return to 'normal', and you will begin dreaming and remembering your dreams nearly every night. This phenomenon can be both exciting and disconcerting for you if you have gone without dreams for an extended period of time. However, the return of dreams it is a sign that your body and mind are healing from the effects of THC and returning to their natural state.

Dreams are an essential part of our cognitive processes, helping us to process emotions, make sense of our experiences, and even problem-solve. By allowing ourselves to dream again, we open up a new world of possibilities and insights that can help us in our daily lives.

Dreaming can also have a positive impact on our emotional well-being. Dreams allow us to explore our deepest fears, desires, and anxieties in a safe and controlled environment, helping us to better understand ourselves and our place in the world. Be prepared for some fascinating and enlightening dreams. Embrace them, learn from them, and use them as a tool for personal growth and self-discovery. You will soon find that your dreams are not just a product of your subconscious, but a vital part of your waking life!

Chapter 7: Boredom & Hobbies

The most common issue after quitting marijuana is boredom. The THC made common basic things in your life exciting and fun. This compounded with having extra money in your pocket and more free time since it is not wasted smoking, you will feel a sense of boredom.

When quitting marijuana, it's common to experience boredom in the first few weeks. This is because activities that once brought you joy no longer feel as enjoyable without THC. However, it's essential to find new ways to engage and entertain yourself without relying on marijuana. Here are some tips on dealing with boredom while going through withdrawal:

Get out of your comfort zone: Try something new that you have never done before. This could be anything from visiting a museum or attending an art class, to trying a new hobby such as painting or gardening. By stepping outside of your comfort zone, you can discover new passions and interests that can help alleviate boredom.

Explore your city: Many people take for granted the beauty and excitement that their city has to offer. Take advantage of this by exploring local parks, museums, and other attractions. You can also attend community events and festivals, which can be both fun and educational.

Call a friend: Reach out to someone who you haven't talked to in a while. Catch up on old times, and plan a day out or activity to do together. Having social support during this time can make a significant difference in reducing feelings of loneliness and boredom.

Read a book: Reading is a great way to stimulate your mind and escape into a different world. Find a genre that interests you, whether it's fiction, mystery, romance, or science-fiction. You can also join a book club to discuss books with others and share your thoughts and opinions.

Volunteer: Giving back to your community can not only benefit others but also give you a sense of purpose. Look for volunteering opportunities in your area and donate your time to a cause you care about. This can be an excellent way to meet new people and learn new skills.

Practice mindfulness: Mindfulness meditation can help reduce stress, anxiety, and boredom. Set aside some time each day to practice deep breathing, relaxation techniques, and guided meditations. This can help calm your mind and body, making it easier to focus on enjoying life without marijuana.

Get moving: Physical exercise is an excellent way to release endorphins, improve mood, and increase energy levels. Consider joining a gym, taking up jogging or cycling, or participating in group fitness classes. Not only will this keep you active, but it can also help you make new friends and connections.

Here are 50 ideas for activities to do to relieve boredom:

1. Take a walk or hike in nature or around the city.
2. Exercise at home or the gym.
3. Try a new recipe and cook a meal.
4. Watch a newly released movie or TV show.
5. Read a book or magazine.
6. Listen to music or podcasts.
7. Play video games, or learn to make video games.
8. Paint or draw.
9. Write in a journal or diary.
10. Learn a new language or programming language.
11. Start a garden.
12. Attend a concert or live event.
13. Visit a museum or art gallery.
14. Go to a comedy club or improv show.
15. Organize your space or declutter.
16. Practice yoga or meditation.
17. Take an online class or course.
18. Plan a trip or vacation.
19. Volunteer at a local charity or organization.
20. Take up a hobby such as knitting or crocheting.
21. Build a model or use LEGO.
22. Create a vision board for your goals.
23. Start a scrapbook or photo album.
24. Make a DIY craft or project.
25. Play a board game or card game.
26. Have a game night with friends.
27. Play sports like basketball, soccer or frisbee.
28. Go dancing or take dance lessons.
29. Have a karaoke night with friends.

30. Join a sports team or league.

31. Start a book club, or find one online.

32. Host a potluck or dinner party.

33. Attend a networking event.

34. Go to trivia night at a bar, brewery, or restaurant.

35. Attend a wine or beer tasting.

36. Go stargazing.

37. Take up photography or astrophotography.

38. Start a blog or subreddit.

39. Attend a poetry reading.

40. Learn a new skill like coding or web design.

41. Write fan fiction or create your own characters.

42. Start a collection of something you love.

43. Attend a festival or fair.

44. Go to an escape room.

45. Take a road trip.

46. Go camping or backpacking.

47. Rent a boat or go on a boat tour.

48. Go fishing or hunting.

49. Try a new type of food or cuisine.

50. Visit a trampoline park or amusement park.

If you find yourself still bored without direction and unsure of what to do, here are 100 additional ideas:

1. Play a board game like Monopoly with friends or family.

2. Start a new hobby: painting, gardening, cooking,

3. Join an online community dedicated to a shared interest.

4. Do creative activities like drawing, writing, or music.

5. Take a class on a topic you're interested in but previously did not have the time for.

6. Rearrange your living area to give it a fresh look and feel.

7. Organize a group outing with friends or family.

8. Participate in a virtual reality experience or simulator

9. Learn a new language through apps, courses, or tutors.

10. Start a writing blog about a topic you know well and enjoy sharing with others.

11. Create a podcast or video series about a subject that interests you.

12. Get involved in volunteer work or social activism to make a positive impact in your community.

13. Arrange a regular game night with friends or family where everyone brings their favorite board game.

14. Host a book club-style discussion group focused on literature, current events, or any other topic of your choice.

15. Begin collecting antiques, art, or other collectible items as a hobby.

16. Write letters to people you care about, old pen pals, or even famous individuals.

17. Join a sports league, recreational team, or fitness center to stay active and social.

18. Attend cultural events, concerts, plays, or museum exhibits both locally and in nearby cities.

19. Study a foreign language by downloading audio books, watching videos, or taking classes online.

20. Engage in meditation or mindfulness practices to clear your mind and find inner peace.

21. Make a list of 100 things to do before you die and track your progress.

22. Start a journal to document your thoughts, experiences, and daily life.

23. Create a vision board with images and symbols representing your goals, dreams, and ideal lifestyle.

24. Enter a contest or competition related to a skill or talent you possess.

25. Learn how to play a musical instrument or dust off an old one and start practicing.

26. Give back to your community by volunteering your time and skills to local charities and organizations.

27. Teach yourself a new skill using YouTube tutorials, online courses, or educational resources.

28. Start a side business based on a hobby or passion project.

29. Create a signature cocktail or dinner entree and share it with friends at a gathering.

30. Practice yoga or join a local yoga studio to improve flexibility and reduce stress.

31. Try a dance class or a new form of exercise to spice up your workout routine.

32. Arrange a weekly dinner night with friends where each person brings the dish they brought to share.

33. Join a book club or reading group to discuss novels and nonfiction books you enjoyed.

34. Set aside time every week to learn more about a topic that interests you.

35. Craft homemade gifts for friends and family using materials from nature or recycled objects.

36. Learn basic coding or a new programming language to expand your knowledge and career options.

37. Start a small business selling handmade crafts or unique items you created.

38. Watch classic movies or television shows you missed the first time around, or binge a show on Netflix/Hulu/etc.

39. Collaborate with other creatives to produce multimedia projects, short films, or podcast episodes.

40. Build a model or replica of something you admire or find interesting.

41. Revive an old hobby, sport, or skill you used to enjoy but let go for some reason.

42. Share your expertise or passions with others through guest lectures, workshops, or webinars.

43. Connect with nature by going on walks, hikes, or camping trips.

44. Develop a signature style in fashion, decorating your home, or personal grooming.

45. Enter a photo contest or exhibit your artwork at local galleries and venues.

46. Start a collection of vinyl records, CDs, or casettes and immerse yourself in the world of audiophile culture.

47. Give presentations or talks on topics you are passionate about or have expertise in.

48. Host regular game nights or movie marathons with friends or family.

49. Explore a new neighborhood or part of town you haven't visited before.

50. Learn about the history of a particular city, region, or country you plan to visit.

51. Research and practice ancient or endangered languages, cultures, and customs.

52. Start a tradition of having themed gatherings with friends for special occasions.

53. Design and print custom t-shirts, posters, or other merchandise featuring your favorite jokes, quotes, or designs.

54. Enter a culinary contest or challenge focusing on a specific cuisine or baking technique.

55. Organize a trash clean-up day in your community to pick up litter and recyclables.

56. Donate your time and skills to help local charities or NGOs working towards causes you care about.

57. Write poetry, short stories, or novel chapters as a way to express yourself creatively.

58. Establish a monthly budget and track your spending to manage your finances better.

59. Create an emergency preparedness kit for your home and vehicle.

60. Learn essential life skills like cooking, sewing, and DIY projects.

61. Make a financial plan for the future including savings, investments, and retirement planning.

62. Organize a clothing swap or donation drive within your circle of friends or community.

63. Become a mentor to someone younger than you who is showing an interest in your area of expertise.

64. Develop a morning routine that includes healthy habits, meditation, and productivity tools.

65. Design a logo for a fictional company or personal brand.

66. Learn about cryptocurrency, blockchain technology, and investing in digital assets.

67. Learn about computer science concepts, programming languages, and software development tools.

68. Create infographics or visually compelling content for social media platforms.

69. Test drive different cars, gadgets, or products you are considering purchasing.

70. Master a new operating system or type of software to boost your job skills.

71. Complete a home improvement project by renovating or updating a room in your house.

72. Redesign or organize spaces in your home, office, or living environment.

73. Network with other professionals in your industry to build connections and learn from their experiences.

74. Learn about the latest tech innovations and developments to keep your skills relevant.

75. Collaborate with other artists, designers, or writers to create joint projects showcasing diverse perspectives.

76. Start a community garden with friends, neighbors, or fellow enthusiasts.

77. Visit historical sites, landmarks, or museums near you to explore your city's rich heritage.

78. Join a gym, fitness center, or sports club to prioritize your physical health.

79. Volunteer with animal shelters, rescue groups, or conservation efforts to support our furry friends.

80. Participate in a road race, fun run, or obstacle course challenges to test your speed, agility, and stamina.

81. Create a virtual reality tour of dream destinations or fantasy worlds to explore without leaving home.

82. Design a personalized planner or notebook layout tailored to your needs and preferences.

83. Learn about alternative energy sources, sustainability, and environmental issues.

84. Start a blog or website dedicated to promoting diversity and inclusion in your field or community.

85. Organize global or national events highlighting underrepresented voices and perspectives.

86. Participate in local theater productions, improv shows, or comedy open mic nights.

87. Perform random acts of kindness or surprise gestures to bring joy to strangers.

88. Complete a photography challenge or a 365-day project to develop your eye for composition and capture moments.

89. Create your own line of personalized merchandise featuring original designs inspired by your passions.

90. Learn about exotic animals, endangered species, and wildlife conservation efforts worldwide.

91. Establish a travel fund or save for dream vacations and adventures to look forward to.

92. Master the art of baking or cooking using specific techniques, ingredients, or culturally authentic recipes.

93. Enter competitions or contests showcasing your artistic, design, or technical abilities.

94. Dabble in the esoteric arts like tarot cards, crystal healing, or astrology.

95. Challenge yourself physically or mentally by attempting circus skills, acrobatic moves, or extreme sport disciplines.

96. Learn about the history of your hometown, state, or country and visit historically significant sites.

97. Teach yourself a new skill or trick by watching videos, joining online communities, or taking free courses.

98. Start a blog or vlog documenting your journey toward self-improvement, weight loss, or sobriety.

99. Create a capsule wardrobe with versatile pieces that can be mixed and matched for effortless everyday styling.

100. Join or create communities dedicated to discussing topics and exchanging ideas with like-minded individuals.

Additionally, here are 45 'writing prompts' that should help keep you busy and distracted:.

1. If you could have dinner with any three people, living or dead, who would they be and why?

2. What is your favorite book and why does it speak to you so much?

3. If you could change one thing about the world, what would it be and why?

4. What is the most challenging thing you've ever done, and what did you learn from it?

5. If you could travel anywhere in the world, where would you go and why?

6. What is your favorite memory from your childhood, and why does it stand out to you?

7. If you could be any animal, which would you choose and why?

8. What is the most valuable lesson you've learned in life so far?

9. If you could witness any event in history, what would it be and why?

10. What is your greatest fear, and how do you cope with it?

11. If you could have any superpower, what would it be and why?

12. What is your favorite season of the year, and why do you love it so much?

13. If you could live in any time period, when would it be and why?

14. What is the most meaningful gift you've ever received, and why was it so special?

15. If you could meet any fictional character, who would it be and why?

16. What is your dream job, and what would you do in that role?

17. If you could erase one mistake you've made, what would it be and why?

18. What is the most important value you hold, and how has it shaped your life?

19. If you could change one thing about yourself, what would it be and why?

20. What is the kindest thing anyone has ever done for you, and why was it so impactful?

21. If you could give advice to your younger self, what would it be?

22. What is the most beautiful place you've ever been, and what made it so stunning?

23. If you could invent something that doesn't currently exist, what would it be and why?

24. What is the most difficult decision you've ever had to make, and how did you arrive at your choice?

25. If you could relive one day from your past, which would it be and why?

26. What is the most inspiring quote you've ever heard, and how has it influenced you?

27. If you could witness a miracle, what would you hope to see?

28. What is the biggest risk you've taken, and how did it turn out?

29. If you could spend a day with a historical figure, who would it be and why?

30. What is the most powerful emotion you've ever felt, and what triggered it?

31. If you could save one endangered species from extinction, which would it be and why?

32. What is the most surprising thing you've ever learned about yourself?

33. If you could eat one meal for the rest of your life, what would it be and why?

34. What is the most fulfilling experience you've ever had, and why was it so gratifying?

35. If you could witness an alien landing on Earth, what would you hope to happen?

36. What is the most challenging question you've ever been asked, and how did you answer it?

37. If you could witness a natural wonder, what would it be and why?

38. What is the most uplifting story you've ever heard, and how did it affect you?

39. If you could witness a scientific breakthrough, what would it be and why?

40. What is the most profound silence you've ever experienced, and why was it so moving?

41. If you could witness a cultural phenomenon, what would it be and why?

42. What is the most exhilarating adventure you've ever embarked on, and why was it so thrilling?

43. If you could witness a moral dilemma, what would it be and how would you resolve it?

44. What is the most creative solution you've ever come up with, and how did you arrive at it?

45. If you could witness a personal triumph, what would it be and why would it be so meaningful?

Or try your hand at art, and draw one of the following:

1.A forest scene with tall trees and a clear sky

2.A bustling cityscape with skyscrapers and cars

3.A serene beach with waves crashing on the shore

4.A snowy mountain landscape with a cozy cabin

5.A busy street with people, shops, and cafes

6.A quiet country road with fields and farmhouses

7.A whimsical fairy garden with flowers and mushrooms

8.A futuristic city with flying cars and buildings

9.A spooky graveyard with old tombstones

10.A peaceful lake with ducks and swans

11.A lush jungle with exotic animals

12.A magical castle with towers and turrets

13.A desert scene with sand dunes and cacti

14.A colorful hot air balloon festival

15.A beautiful sunset over the ocean

16.A mystical cave with glowing crystals

17.A vibrant marketplace with stalls and vendors

18.A charming village with cobblestone streets

19.A haunted mansion with ghostly apparitions

20.A beautiful rose garden with blooming flowers

21.A medieval town with a castle and knights

22. A pirate ship sailing on the high seas
23. A dinosaur park with prehistoric creatures
24. A space station with astronauts and aliens
25. A train ride through the countryside
26. A circus with acrobats and clowns
27. A carnival with games and rides
28. A zoo with animals from around the world
29. A botanical garden with rare plants
30. A museum with ancient artifacts
31. A mermaid lagoon with coral reefs
32. A robot factory with machines and gears
33. A dreamy underwater scene with sea creatures
34. A steampunk city with steam-powered machines
35. A fantasy world with dragons and elves

"Don't watch the clock; do what it does. Keep going." - Sam Levenson

Chapter 8: Staying off THC

By the 6 month mark, you will be able to look back on your recent months without THC and notice your brain healing and restoring itself, resulting in increased self-confidence, better decision-making abilities, and improved relationships. Your body has also adjusted to the absence of THC, leading to clearer skin, stronger immune system, and reduced risk of lung issues. Take note of how much money you have saved not purchasing THC products, and how much time you have saved by not having to drive to a dispensary or dealer to purchase it.

At one year without marijuana, you have established a new routine free from the habits associated with using marijuana. you will notice positive changes in your physical appearance, such as weight loss or muscle gain due to increased exercise and better nutrition. You have literally helped your body de-age, you look younger and you have likely added years to your expected life simply by quitting.

There may be times when you are tempted to use marijuana again, even just for one quick puff. However, it is essential to resist this temptation and stay committed to your *clarity*. The first step in overcoming temptation is to understand the reasons behind it. Are you feeling stressed or anxious? Are you experiencing withdrawal symptoms like irritability or cravings? Identifying the root cause of your temptation can help you develop effective coping mechanisms to deal with these challenges.

It is also crucial to 'actually do stuff' during periods of temptation. Engage in activities that bring you joy and relaxation, such as exercise, learning, or spending time outside. These activities can help reduce stress levels and improve overall well-being, making it easier to resist the urge to start using it again.

Finally, remember that every day of *clarity* is a victory worth celebrating. Take time to acknowledge your progress and reflect on the positive changes you have made in your life. Keep track of your accomplishments by writing down milestones. This can provide much-needed motivation and inspiration when the temptations arise.

"The greatest glory in living lies not in never falling, but in rising every time we fall."

Chapter 9: Resources & Support

The focus of this book has been quitting marijuana on your own, but it should be noted that there are some *fantastic* online groups and resources should you need support or want to help support others on their *Rise to Clarity*.

www.reddit.com/r/leaves/[1]

Reddit's r/leaves community is the #1 online resource for providing support and encouragement to those looking to quit THC. With over 350,000 members, this subreddit is dedicated to helping people who want to stop using cannabis. Members can participate in discussions, share personal stories, ask questions, and receive advice from others who have gone through or are currently going through the same struggles, such as dealing with withdrawal symptoms, finding alternative coping mechanisms, and maintaining long-term sobriety.

One of the key features of /r/leaves/ is its daily check-in thread, where users can report their progress and hold themselves accountable for their goals. This practice fosters a sense of community and encouragement among members, as they can celebrate each other's successes and provide motivation during challenging times. Additionally, many users choose to

---

1.   http://www.reddit.com/r/leaves/

share personal stories about their addiction and recovery process, which can be both inspiring and educational for others. These posts often highlight the negative consequences of marijuana use and demonstrate how quitting has led to improved mental health, relationships, and overall quality of life.

/r/leaves/ also offers a wealth of resources and tools to help people on their journey toward sobriety. For example, the subreddit maintains a comprehensive list of recommended books, podcasts, documentaries, and websites that provide valuable information about marijuana addiction and recovery. Moderators regularly post motivational quotes, articles, and infographics to inspire and educate members. By curating these resources, /r/leaves/ serves as an invaluable hub for those seeking guidance and support during their recovery process.

Another crucial aspect of /r/leaves/ is its strong emphasis on harm reduction and aftercare. Many users discuss various strategies for managing cravings and urges, such as engaging in hobbies, practicing mindfulness, and reaching out to supportive friends. /r/leaves fosters an inclusive and non-judgmental atmosphere where individuals from all backgrounds can feel safe sharing their experiences and seeking support. The community actively promotes respectful dialogue and discourages stigmatizing language or negative stereotypes about marijuana addiction and recovery. This inclusive environment allows members to form genuine connections and build supportive relationships with others who understand their struggles firsthand. Check it out sometime!

www.reddit.com/r/leaves/

Chapter 10: Final Thoughts

Thank you for taking the time to read this book and to empower yourself with the knowledge needed to quit marijuana habits. Using this knowledge you can now have a vastly improved life in all areas, and you now have the ability to help others on their journey towards a THC-free lifestyle. I hope that you will recommend this book to others, and pass along what you have learned to others who may be struggling with marijuana addiction.

Throughout history, numerous individuals have faced the challenge of quitting marijuana habits. By examining these stories, we can gain valuable insights into the strategies employed by successful individuals in their quest for sobriety. One notable example is the story of Bob Marley, who battled his own marijuana addiction before ultimately overcoming it through a combination of personal determination, self-reflection, and support from loved ones. Another inspiring figure is former NBA player Chris Herren, who openly shares his experiences with substance abuse in order to raise awareness and help others on their path to recovery. Music legend Snoop Dog quit smoking due to health issues. Brad Pitt, Paul McCartney, Lady Gaga, Miley Cyrus, Jennifer Lawrence, Woody Harrelson, and many more celebrities have been public about their struggle to ditch marijuana - they have all quit and are currently living their life with *clarity* - and now so are *you.*